BEYOND BOOM AND CRASH

Robert L. Heilbroner

BEYOND BOOM
AND CRASH

W·W·NORTON & COMPANY, INC·
New York

Much of the material in this book appeared originally in *The New Yorker.*

Library of Congress Cataloging in Publication Data

Heilbroner, Robert L.
  Beyond boom and crash.

  Includes index.
  1. Economic history—1945–   2. Capitalism.
3. Business cycles. 4. Depressions. I. Title.
HC59.H378 1978 330.9′04 78–17846
ISBN 0–393–05707–0

  2 3 4 5 6 7 8 9 0

for my Shirley

Acknowledgments

I am indebted to David Gordon for implanting the original idea from which this lengthy essay developed and to Harold van B. Cleveland and David Calleo for discussions that advanced it toward its present shape. None of the above had any idea that he was contributing to the final product, but I would like nonetheless to acknowledge my indebtedness to them. As so often before, I have relied on the advice of Adolph Lowe and Peter Bernstein; and as so often before it has been indispensable.

BEYOND BOOM AND CRASH

I

ANOTHER WORLDWIDE crisis of capitalism is upon us. Why it has appeared and what consequences it portends for the economic system in which we live are the questions I wish to consider here. But first, we should take note that it is *another* crisis of capitalism. From its earliest days, capitalism has always been as critically ill as it has been intensely alive. "Convulsions" and "revulsions," as the older political economists called them, "crises," as Marx identified them, "recessions" and "depressions," in modern economic language, have been as prominent features of capitalist development as its dizzying succession of technical advances, its enormous material productivity, its irresistible global expansion. So there is nothing new in the fact of crisis. Indeed, by comparison with some past crises, above all the catastrophe of the 1930s, the present seizure has been mild.

Nonetheless, it *is* a crisis, and, as always before, it has brought a sense of ominous foreboding. If the economic history of capitalism is one of boom and bust, its psychological history is one of alternating confidence and despair. Even a relatively mild crisis, where social disruption is minimal, brings specters of collapse, revolution, the end of the world. Hence this is a good time to look into the etiology of capitalist crisis as a kind of chronic disease of the system and to venture whatever prognosis seems possible.

Economists, like doctors, should begin with case histories. In the present instance, there is no doubt that the patient seemed in extraordinarily good health prior to his attack. The years from 1950 to the early 1970s were the longest period of growth that capitalism had ever experienced, almost a quarter century of nearly uninterrupted expansion. Moreover, the expansion was shared among all capitalist nations, without exception. Germany and Japan enjoyed rates of economic growth that doubled their real incomes every seven years. France shook off a history of chronic stagnation to emerge as a modern industrial power. Italy

12

managed to overcome horrendous unemployment and dislocation to achieve a dazzling, if uneven, prosperity —from "Bicycle Thief" to "La Dolce Vita" in twenty years. Sweden surpassed the per capita income of the United States. And even our own country, weighed down with the costs of a terrible war and a near-rebellious young and black population, managed to attain an entirely new level of material well-being. By 1970 the average household enjoyed an income about three-quarters larger in real terms than in 1950.

Then came the crisis. Beginning in some countries in late 1973, in others during the following year, the long trend of growth came to an abrupt halt. In the United States, output declined by nine percent from 1974 to 1975. In Germany and France, production fell by a percentage point less; in Italy and Japan by a percentage point more. In Canada, Sweden, Norway, Denmark, the Netherlands, Austria, Australia, Hong Kong, Mexico, the Union of South Africa, Israel, Spain, and Portugal—in short, in every nation with a predominantly capitalist economy—the crisis appeared, varying in extent from one to the next, but visible in all.

The extent was never of panic proportions—in the Great Depression in the United States, output fell by nearly fifty percent from its peak in 1929 to its nadir in 1933. Nothing resembling such a collapse attended the crisis of the early 1970s. The sharpest decline was probably a 13 percent slide in Japan from 1973 to

13

1975. Nevertheless, the crisis brought its toll. In the United States unemployment rose by three-quarters between 1973 and 1975, far short of the eightfold increase during the Great Depression, but enough to disemploy eight percent of all "experienced" workers and to create pockets of unemployment that ran up to ninety percent of black adolescent job seekers in some ghetto areas. In Europe the problem was less severe because the European boom had utilized the labor of imported mercenaries, mainly from Yugoslavia, Greece, and Turkey. When the boom stopped, these recruits to the labor army were shipped home in large numbers. Nonetheless, production fell sufficiently so that unemployment among native Germans and Frenchmen and Britons became a social and political issue for the first time in twenty years.

Following that global downturn, almost all capitalist economies have recovered to a considerable degree. Japan reversed its decline within a year. By early 1978, in most of Europe, production was about four or five percent above precrisis levels; only England failed to regain its former peak. In the United States, output was by then about 7 percent above precollapse levels, and unemployment had fallen by about a fifth from its peak, although it was still seriously worse than in 1973. In Europe the unemployment issue remained live, but not charged. Only in the peripheral countries, to which the "guest workers" returned, was it a heavy burden, but these were countries with relatively large

14

rural work forces and with networks of extended families, all of which absorb and "hide" unemployment.

Thus there is a good deal of evidence that the crisis that began in 1973 has been weathered and that a resumption of the upward trend, although perhaps at a somewhat slower pace, has already commenced. Yet a sense of an unliquidated problem lingers on. The price of gold continues to be high, testimony to the beliefs of investors around the world as to the unreliability of stocks and bonds and conventional money. The dollar has become a currency that foreign banks or governments will no longer hold in unlimited amounts. Stock exchanges in every nation are well below their precrisis peaks. Books like the *The Crash of '79*, prophesying complete financial breakdown, exert a fascination that suggests and perhaps breeds belief. The talk in financial circles is of another crisis ahead; of long-term structural problems that are barely recognized, much less overcome; of a European community that is fighting demoralization; of an American economy unable to generate momentum; of an inflation that no one even pretends to be able to manage; of the need for a "real" depression to cleanse the system—provided that it does not do it in.

How much truth there may lie in these dark forebodings is a matter we shall consider in due course. But first we must complete the patient's history. For unlike most crises in the past where the precipitating factor is beyond discovery—we know, of course, that

15

Robert L. Heilbroner

the stock market crash ticked off the Great Depression, but we do not know what precipitated the crash—we can identify the immediate cause of the 1973–74 "revulsion." This was the sudden increase in the price of oil by the Organization of Petroleum Exporting Countries (OPEC) in the fall of 1973, after the Israeli-Arab conflict broke out. Within a few months the price of oil quadrupled, and the capitalist oil-using nations found themselves facing an annual bill for petroleum in excess of $100 billion.

The consequences were a shockwave of alarm. "A landslide of immense proportions is rumbling downhill toward most of the oil-consuming industrialized world," wrote *The Economist*, ". . . a landslide capable of breaking the financial system and the economies of several major countries." Unquestionably, oil shock triggered the initial crisis. But the continuing high price of oil is by no means responsible for the oppressive mood that remains. The Arab nations did not, as feared, sit on their immense oil proceeds, but exerted every effort to recycle the money back into Western hands. A sheer physical shortage of oil, of the kind that caused lines at gas pumps during the brief period of the oil embargo, was never repeated; in fact, by 1978 there was a surplus of oil looking for buyers at the high prices maintained by the OPEC cartel. More evidence that oil was not responsible for the refusal of the crisis to dissipate itself could be seen in the quick recovery of Japan, the most vulnerable of all the oil importers,

16

and the persistent sluggishness of England, a capitalist economy that actually developed its own oil resources since the OPEC crisis. (Norway, which shared in the North Sea oil field, also experienced a recession, despite its oil revenues.)

Thus oil shock can be blamed for the onset of the worldwide capitalist crisis, but not for its subsequent history. Rather, it seems clear that oil precipitated the present global recession much as the Great Crash of Wall Street precipitated the depression of the 1930s. In both cases, the system itself seems to be the cause of the trouble, giving way like an overstrained structure subjected to a telling blow. But why was the system overstrained? Why did not the immense expansive power of the twenty-five-year boom reassert itself in full force? How real are the specters that still haunt Wall Street and its European counterparts?*

*Notes and comments on each section begin on page 91.

II

SUCH QUESTIONS take us backstage to consider how capitalism as a system generates economic growth in the first place. Here I find it useful to adopt a view of the economy first described by Marx. Marx depicts the process much as a businessman would —namely, as the complicated way in which money makes money and business capital expands.

Marx pictures this as a great accumulation "circuit" that can be divided into three distinct phases or stages. In the first phase, businessmen hire labor and buy the

18

raw or semifinished goods needed to start up production. In other words, they turn their money capital into labor power and supplies of various kinds. Moreover, if their business is to grow, they must turn ever *more* money into labor power and materials. Generalized to include the entire system, this means that a growing economy requires the hiring of more and more labor, and the buying of larger and larger quantities of materials, not only to turn out more consumable goods, but also to build new plant and equipment, the process economists call investment.

This initial phase of Marx's "circuit" of accumulation immediately identifies two potential sources of crisis. The first is the crucial role played by business-men's expectations. If capitalists do not anticipate growth—if the state of business confidence is poor—they will not invest in additional plant and equipment, and may not even seek to convert all their existing cash into payrolls and supplies. That is a problem to which we will return later, for expectations obviously play a critical role in determining the pace of advance or in determining whether there will be *any* advance.

But a second obstacle, of no less importance, also resides in the first stage. Money will not even begin its tortuous journey through the system if a labor force cannot be hired, or if supplies of materials or plant and equipment are not available. When workers strike, capitalist growth comes to a total halt, at least insofar as that particular portion of the economy is concerned.

19

For the system as a whole this stoppage may be trivial, as when a small local union goes on strike, but it can also bring to a halt a very large section of industry.

Of course it is not only a strike that can paralyze the initial phase in which money seeks to "become" labor power and materials. If workers are unwilling to work at the wages that employers want to pay, the circuit is interrupted as effectively as if there were a strike. Or if needed inputs are unavailable or too expensive, the circuit is cut just as effectively as by the high price of labor. The OPEC oil shock was precisely such an event —a blow to the first phase of the accumulation process sufficiently severe to bring about a marked reduction in the scale of activity in every industrial nation.

Let us suppose, however, that money-capital is successfully converted into payrolls and stocks of materials and equipment. This now brings us to the second phase of the production process as Marx describes it— a part of the circuit located entirely within the factory rather than in the marketplace. Here no money is directly involved. Rather, the money that has been turned into labor power, raw materials, and other necessities for production is now further turned into the finished products that will emerge from the factory gate. Labor energies, and the physical and chemical properties of the materials and equipment with which labor works, now make steel out of iron, gasoline out of petroleum, cloth out of yarn.

And here again a set of potential obstacles to the

accumulation process must be surmounted. Labor must perform its tasks efficiently and in a disciplined fashion. The engineering processes must function smoothly. Raw materials must be of proper grade and kind. Obviously the difficulties encountered in this second phase of the circuit are of a different nature than those of the first. Interruptions to labor discipline, such as absenteeism, sabotage, "work-to-rule" slowdowns, vandalism, or indifference will damage the process by which money, embodied in labor power and materials, becomes transformed into salable outputs. The morale problems that have plagued American and European factories in recent years, of which the obstreperous Lordstown plant of General Motors was for a time a national symbol, are illustrations of the interruptions we encounter in the second stage. So are disruptions to the flow of production when raw materials are below grade, or goods in process defective, or plant and machinery inadequate. To the extent that the ability of a company to sell its products is damaged by a reputation for poor workmanship, the ability of that company to recoup its money-capital is hurt as severely as if a strike had shut its plants. Generalized to a sufficient degree (as in the automobile industry, where poor engineering and sloppy work have forced the recall of millions of cars), the problems of the second phase of the circuit of accumulation can threaten the profitability of an entire industry.

Finally, there is the third phase, the one most famil-

21

iar to businessmen and economists alike. This is the phase in which capital, now embodied in a finished good, must complete its metamorphosis back into money. The metamorphosis takes place by selling the good, an act that commands the principal attention of the business world, although we can now see that selling is only the last, and not necessarily the most critical, of the links in the chain.

The obstacles faced in this third stage are again of a different kind than those of the previous ones. Changes in buyers' wants or needs, whether the consequence of changes in fashion or technology, can reduce the value of output to a fraction of its expected worth. Events over which an individual business has no control—indeed, events over which the collective business world, or the nation-state itself, have no control—can cause markets to disappear into thin air, or on occasion can create profitable sales opportunities out of equally thin air. Thus the process of completing the circle of capital accumulation by selling the output of business is always attended by anxiety and uncertainty. In one way or another it is essential that the last loop of the process be closed if business is to recoup its original money outlays, but closing that loop is often difficult and sometimes impossible.

III

THUS THREE SEPARATE obstacle courses must be negotiated if capital, in the form of money, is to return to its original hands, ready for still another round of metamorphoses. In view of the complexity and the dangers of these successive stages, our first reaction is to wonder how the process can ever be completed at all. Rather than accounting for the recurrent fact of crises—that is, of breakdowns somewhere in the system—the burden seems shifted: how, we ask, can can such a labyrinthine journey hope to be safely undertaken, not once, but again and again, as part of the "mechanism" of the system?

The answer lies in becoming aware that the mechanism is not some kind of tutelary deity that smiles over the capitalist process, but is lodged in the living, breathing—often very hard breathing—bodies of millions of persons whose full-time endeavor is to *make* the process work. For example, the initial process by which money is turned into labor power and materials is successfully concluded only because workers and their union leaders are as eager to come to terms with employers as employers are with them. The labor market in which hiring takes place is motivated by pressures of need as well as greed, of aspiration as well as defeat. Labor and capital come together as iron filings to the pole of a magnet, each "particle" of labor drawn to an employer, and the "pole" of capital drawn to the mass of workers. So too, similar efforts bring together the suppliers of raw materials and equipment with the firms who must spend money to procure them. Purchasing agents, brokers, executives of both buying and selling concerns, all spend their energies in finding supplies of materials of the right kind and price so that production may begin.

The same outpouring of energy seeks to assure the completion of the production stage, where labor and materials are joined to create goods for sale. This is the domain of the foreman, the efficiency expert, the personnel manager, and the production boss. Here is where Ph.D.s trained in psychology seek to remove obstacles of behavior, while other Ph.D.s, trained in engineering and business management, seek to remove those of space, time, and organization; where union shop stewards and local managers work to prevent grievances from exploding into disruptions to the work process, and safety engineers install precautionary devices to prevent accidents from slowing or stopping production lines; where statistical sampling procedures detect variations in the quality of output before it is too late, and computer printouts inform men in shirtsleeves whether the rivers of subassemblies are advancing in proper coordination. Thus, like the metamorphosis of money into labor power and goods, the interaction of labor power with goods takes place not by the workings of a mysterious "mechanism," but because it is the object of the intense concern, attention, expertise, and will of millions of individuals.

The same is true again when we reach the final stage in which commodities turn back into money, like frogs into princes. This time, of course, the process takes place as the consequence of an army of persons concerned with selling—copywriters, television actors with stentorian voices, models with pretty faces, merchandisers with clever ideas, ordinary sales clerks behind counters. At the same time, this crucial final closure of the total circuit is also expedited by two other extremely important groups who anxiously superintend the process at a remove. One consists of the financial institutions—banks, finance companies, savings and loan associations—who help complete the closure (as they also help business initiate it in the first phase) by lending buyers money. Second is the government, watching anxiously over the confused process in which all three loops of the capital-regeneration process are inextricably intertwined. Although the government intervenes at many points in all three stages, its main attention is fixed on the buying power of the households and businesses who must create princes by waving the magic wand of money. By its fiscal and monetary policies—that is, by raising and lowering expenditures and taxes, or by adjusting the supply of money—the government tries mightily to assure that the wand is waved and the process brought to a successful termination, prior to its instant recommencement. Thus, at the apex of the economy, as at its base, the economy "works" because an enormous fraction of the total life energies and intelligence of society is devoted to making it work.

IV

WHEN WE LOOK at the process of capitalist growth in this fashion, the question changes once more: how can the process *fail* to work? When so much energy and intelligence, drive and adaptation go into the various subprocesses that constitute the whole, how can the accumulation process falter?

One reason, of course, is that the actors who strive so earnestly can make mistakes. If they are small mistakes, they cancel out, one person's shortfall balanced by another's windfall. From time to time very large

27

mistakes are made, and huge enterprises go under because they cannot begin production, or because they are unable to discipline the work process, or through a failure of marketing. Then the Edsel fails, or the Pennsylvania Railroad goes bankrupt, or the Lockheed Company totters.

But as these instances illustrate, even giant failures do not create more than temporary pauses in the ongoing accumulation process of the entire economy. A more likely candidate for the role of villain is mistaken or wrong-headed action taken by the government itself. In the 1930s, for example, the Federal Reserve Board deliberately tightened the money supply, making it difficult for banks to resume their lending operations, because the Board was obsessed with a fear of inflation, despite the fact that a quarter of the work force was unemployed. In so doing it was probably the single most important contributory element in the persistent failure of the economy to resume its forward momentum.

In more recent years recessions have actually been deliberately initiated in Washington, the fear of inflation taking precedence over a concern for unemployment—the difference being that the Federal Reserve in the 1930s knew not what it wrought, whereas the Administration in 1974 knew very well what it was doing. In similar fashion, a considerable part of the explanation for the poor performance of the American (and most European) economies after "oil shock" was the imposition of conscious monetary restraints by governments seeking to put a halt to inflation, even at the expense of recession, or indeed by the very means of an engineered recession.

We shall subsequently have more to say about the role of government in managing or mismanaging inflation, but the answer to our question does not lie in the upsetting presence of "mistakes" or deliberate recessionary policy. Capitalist economies have encountered regular crises long before governments were meddling in the economic process, and the collapses of giant firms, usually in finance, generally took place as a consequence, rather than as a direct cause, of recessions. Thus we shall have to search elsewhere for explanations of the recurrence of crisis. Indeed, we shall have to see if we cannot find causes for crisis that are the outgrowth of the very success of capitalist growth.

One such endemic "counterprocess" is relatively easy to locate. It is the inherent spoiling effect of a period of boom on the labor and materials markets of the first phase of the accumulation process. For the more successful is this first phase—the more steadily money becomes transformed into labor power and goods—the more do the prices of labor and materials tend to rise. As Adam Smith already saw, the accumulation of wealth bids up the price of labor, and as David Ricardo added, it also raises the price of any

29

other commodity whose supply cannot be quickly increased, or whose supply can be increased only at higher cost.

Thus the successful completion of the first stage tends to tighten loose markets—for labor, materials, space, money—because the growing demand for the factors of production tends to raise their prices. As every businessman knows, booms jack up costs. Rising costs in turn squeeze business income. As the pressure against profits mounts, the general enthusiasm of the early days of the boom gives way to a growing unease about labor's "demands" and raw materials' prices.

As the squeeze intensifies, the willingness or the ability to go on producing declines. Businesses cancel plans for expansion as too expensive. They decide to hang onto their money rather than to risk it in the accumulation process. The process begins to falter. A recession is at hand.

There is, I must emphasize, nothing mechanical or certain about this. A tight labor market may be relieved if cheap labor can be imported from abroad, or if automation can be quickly introduced. A rise in materials' prices may simply lead to the use of substitutes or the rapid exploitation of new sources of supply. Credit shortages can be eased by government policy. Or the business outlook may remain buoyant, despite a rise in costs, because businessmen are convinced that "they" won't allow a recession to occur. In a word, expansion can continue in the face of rising

costs, or rising costs may themselves set into motion
corrective processes that temper the rise in wages and
prices. (Adam Smith pointed out that a rise in wages
would enable more of the child labor force to stay
alive, thereby offsetting the increased demand for
labor by an increased supply of it.)

So there is nothing in the self-spoiling propensities
of a successful boom that is certain to abort the overall
circuit of capital accumulation. Rather, a *potential* for
disruption lies in the tendency of a boom to raise prices
and thereby to constrict profits. Whether such a potential constriction *actually* takes place hinges on innumer-
able circumstances and cannot be predicted. It is
enough to recognize that it could.

A second source of disruption, likewise rooted in
the success of the accumulation process, lies within the
second phase, where labor power and materials are
combined to create salable commodities. Here the
problem has nothing to do with money. It is to be
found in the difficulty of maintaining a smooth flow of
production during an extended period of prosperity.

In turn, this difficulty rests on the nature of the labor
process within industrial capitalism (and, indeed,
within the forms of industrial socialism that are heirs
to this labor process). Industrial labor requires an ex-
traordinary amount of discipline. This is because labor
under capitalism is systematically reduced to what
Marx called "detail labor"—the performance of oper-

ations that have no significance in themselves, but are important only as units of a larger whole. Industrial production requires the steady, coordinated, dependable performance of tasks each one of which has little or no meaning, aesthetic satisfaction, tradition, art, pleasure, or completion. Compared with the work of artisans, or even of peasant farmers, the work of men and women in factories and offices is fragmented, pointless, empty of intrinsic meaning, however much money it may earn for its protagonist. (This is probably what Marx meant when he said that the worker under capitalism became ever more "impoverished," whether his wage was high or low.)

To perform this labor with the machinelike regularity on which the production process as a whole depends requires that men and women submit to a routine that few do not find irksome. In the main the great majority of working people *do* submit, partly from the need to earn a living, partly from the social pressure to conform, partly from the absence of any imaginable alternative. But the irksomeness of the work process, like a hair shirt, is never lost to consciousness. And when prosperity continues, and the bargaining position and economic security of working people improve, the necessary discipline becomes harder to obtain. Absenteeism increases. Unions demand and get more job perks. Wildcat strikes break out over trifles. The authority of foremen diminishes. The issue of "work satisfaction" comes to the fore.

It is clear that a very large potential for the interruption of capitalist accumulation resides in the lurking indiscipline of the labor process. General strikes are unknown in this country, but are all too familiar abroad, where they have on occasion paralyzed England, France, Italy, Austria, the Netherlands, Sweden, and other nations. Even in countries that lack a unified and militant labor force, the problem of indiscipline is an ever present threat to the smooth regeneration of capital. Moreover, the threat of indiscipline worsens as the general prosperity of the work force improves, and bright prospects for employment elsewhere encourage labor to express its dissatisfactions. Consequently, we find efforts to lessen the irksomeness of labor by breaking up the monotony of assembly lines, as in the famous Volvo team system first tried in Sweden and now being used in a number of firms elsewhere; or to instill a sense of self-respect through trim uniforms, piped-in music, "personalized" cubicles, special training for foremen in the dynamics of group psychology, company sports, outings, and morale-building activities. The effort to overcome the problem of labor indiscipline is probably most fully expressed in Japanese firms that begin the day with mass calisthenics and singing, and that provide lessons in flower arranging for their female employees, as well as guaranteeing lifetime employment (after a relatively short apprenticeship), provided that the employee does not give "cause" for dismissal.

A third, separate source of potential difficulty, also generated by the boom itself, lies in the last of the three phases of the accumulation process, where commodities must be converted into money. Here the difficulty is simply stated. It is that production tends to glut markets. Goods come off assembly lines faster than consumers can absorb them. Inventories pile up. Eventually, production has to be cut back.

Every businessman knows that gluts can spoil individual markets. The great question—one that has been debated in economics for a century and a half—is whether there can be "general gluts," gluts for everything. Most economists today say no, that total demand is for all intents and purposes limitless and insatiable, spreading out from necessities toward infinite luxuries.

The problem of the third phase, however, is not one of spoiling total demand. It is rather that an economy that has enjoyed a boom may find it very difficult to rearrange production to suit the changing patterns of demand as *particular* markets get filled up. Production processes that are city blocks long and months "deep" are not easily switched off or turned around. Gluts for products such as automobiles or ships or planes or export crops lead to pockets of unused labor and equipment that cannot be rapidly redeployed to meet other possible demands. These pockets become centers of depression whose infectious power is very great.

In addition, there is the larger problem of matching

demand against supply, not just in one market or another, but in terms of the total amount of purchasing power generated back in phase one and the total value of goods produced in phase two. Here the question is not one of glut, but one of a balance between buying power and *expected* revenues. Perhaps all the existing output can be sold, but if it must be unloaded at prices less favorable than were originally hoped for, the expectations that drive the accumulation process will receive a setback. It is also true that if goods are sold at prices greater than those originally hoped for, business will receive a very strong stimulus. Thus the matching of buying power, on the one hand, and expected revenues on the other, holds out the possibility of disappointments that can lead to reduced production, or of windfalls that can lead to increased prices. In the phrase of Sir Roy Harrod, the eminent English economist who first formulated the difficulties of achieving "balanced growth," capitalism walks a "knife edge" between recession on one side and inflation on the other.

Thus the third phase of the overall process of capitalist reproduction and growth is a center of constant tragedy and near-tragedy, as well as of triumph or lucking-out. Gluts, or mismatches between supply and demand, are the stuff of everyday market life, as the business pages of any newspaper will testify, and a vast amount of effort goes into seeking to avert or rescue such gluts through sales, write-downs, write-offs, promotions, and the like. On a larger scale, the mismatch of whole sectors of outputs, such as crops or raw materials or housing, may lead to government intervention to prevent disasters from spreading. And, not least, the fiscal and monetary authorities are constantly scanning the economic scene for indications of mismatches between the volume of production and the volume of money incomes, with consequences that we will examine in our next section.

The difficulties of the third phase, like those of the first two, do not dictate an "inevitable" breakdown. It would be better to say that gluts, either for particular sectors or on a larger scale, are the principal reason for shortcircuits in this last of the three distinguishable stages of accumulation. They result in what Marx called "realization crises"—failures to "realize" the capital tied up in commodities because they cannot be sold at profitable prices.

The above is not, of course, anything like a full description of the causes of economic crisis, much less a systematic tracing through the interconnections by which crises exert their effects. But it must be clear that the susceptibility to crisis lies directly within the process of capitalist expansion itself. It is the success of the system—its solution to the problem of converting money into goods and labor, and then reconverting the resultant production into new money, that increases the tension of the accumulative process. The tension is eventually snapped by a change in expectations or behavior, or in physical or social realities, somewhere along the lengthy path of money making. Crisis thus appears to be not so much an exceptional occurence as an event whose appearance is to be expected, although one never quite knows where or when. The system is crisis-prone not because it cannot make its subcircuits operate, but because the very act of successfully operating them creates tensions that make the economy vulnerable to breakdown.

V

ONE LAST MATTER needs to be put into the picture: An even larger cause of the instability of the capitalist world during the last twenty years has been the problem of inflation.

Inflation has become so widely accepted as an inevitable aspect of economic life that it comes as something of a surprise to recall that it was not inflation but deflation—falling prices—that was the primary problem in the earlier history of capitalism. Between 1823 and 1848, for example, wholesale prices in the United

States fell by twenty-five percent. They were pushed upward by the Civil War, but again between 1873 and 1898 prices fell by almost fifty percent, so that at the end of the nineteenth century they were actually below the level of 1823, the Civil War notwithstanding. The same was true elsewhere. In England, for instance, wholesale prices fell from the 1870s until the turn of the century. In Germany, as well, the level of wholesale prices in 1910 was below that of 1880.

Bursts of inflation always appeared with the advent of war, and during some decades prices drifted gently upwards. But nothing like the phenomenon that we have come to accept as "normal" appears until after World War II. Then, beginning in the early 1950s, after the wreckage of the war was cleared away, we discern an international upward creep, averaging no more than 2.5 percent a year, on the average, until 1960. Thereafter the creep became a trot. From 1960 to 1970, the average rate of inflation for the ten major capitalist nations rose to 4.1 percent a year. Then it quickened further. From 1970 to 1975 the rate went to 8.0 percent a year.

In this worldwide phenomenon, the experience of the United States has been considerably less severe than that of most other capitalist economies. Taking the period as a whole, we have had one of the world's lowest inflation rates (along with West Germany and Canada). Although our rate of inflation exceeded that of the other major industrial nations in the years between 1968 and 1970, if we sum up our experience from 1968 to early 1978, we discover that, whereas our consumer prices went up by 86 percent, French prices were up 121 percent, Japanese prices 145 percent, Italian prices 172 percent, English prices 202 percent. Only West Germany has been markedly less inflationary than we. Prices over the same period increased there by only 58 percent.

It is often said that there is no "theory" of inflation, comparable to that which John Maynard Keynes provided for the analysis of depression. In a way that is true; in a way not. Keynes revealed how it was possible for an economy to remain in a condition of equilibrium—that is, without any tendency to move—even though its level of output was so low that large numbers of men and vast amounts of machinery and equipment were unemployed and unutilized. Keynes's theory was thus an explanation of the reasons that prevented a market economy from attaining the level of activity to which its profit-seeking capitalists and employment-seeking work force seemed otherwise certain to drive it. (His explanation hinged on the powerful role played by pessimistic expectations in causing businessmen to curtail or inhibit their spending for expansion). It was, therefore, a theory that explained how a stable condition of less-than-full employment was compatible with the expansive propensities of the protagonists of the system, a state of affairs that had appeared "impossible" to the analysts of the pre-Keynesian era.

But Keynes's theory was not an explanation of the *cause* of depression. That is, it did not identify the specific reasons why business expectations should be disappointed. Keynes stressed the crucial role played by business spending for investment in propelling the economy forward, and he added the vital understanding that this flow of spending could be more or less indefinitely depressed if businessmen could not anticipate adequate future earnings. But he did not discover reasons, either outside the economy or within its normal operations, that would induce such a state of frustrated hopes. Neither did he explain what might be the cause of the regular bouts of pessimism that affected the economy, depressing its investment activities every seven to ten years with the rhythm of the business "cycle."

With regard to inflation, curiously enough, we are today in a position that is more or less the direct opposite of Keynes's. When it comes to understanding the process of inflation—the mechanisms by which inflation is accelerated or reined in—we have nothing like our Keynesian understanding of how depressions are sustained, or worsened, or relieved. On the other hand, whereas Keynes does not enlighten us much about the initiating causes of depression, we have at least a general grasp of the

41

reasons why inflation has come to dominate the
Western capitalist world.

When we look at the historical picture, the root
cause of the inflationary phenomenon suggests itself
immediately. It is a change that profoundly distin-
guishes modern capitalism from the capitalism of the
prewar era—the presence of a government sector
vastly larger and far more intimately enmeshed in the
process of capitalist growth than can be discovered
anywhere prior to World War II.

The United States offers a convenient illustration
here. In 1929, government buying provided about 7
percent of our gross national product (the conventional measure of aggregate economic activity), while
business spending for investment provided nearly
twice as much, or 13 percent. By 1970, government
buying amounted to roughly 20 percent of GNP, not
quite half again as large as business investment. And
if we add to government buying of output, the enormous "transfer" expenditures made by government,
such as social security payments (which do not pur-
chase output in the same manner as government buying of military or educational services), the transformation is much more striking. In 1929 the ratio of
government spending for all purposes to gross national
product was about 8 percent. Today it is roughly 30
percent. This change is even more dramatically evi-
denced in Europe, where the percentage of gross na-

tional product that flows through government, either as purchases of output or as transfers of income, goes over fifty percent in a number of nations.

No less fundamentally altered is the role of government within the economy. Prior to World War II, governments tended to be passive agents in the ebb and flow of economic affairs, with the main exception of their responsibility for establishing a favorable exchange rate for their currencies and protecting their industries by tariffs or other trade arrangements. The world of international affairs aside, governments did not think of themselves as possessing either the right or the capacity to affect the process of capitalist accumulation itself. Economic policy was therefore limited to measures whose objective was always quite specific—to aid this business group or that region, this promising interest or that strategic one. When crisis came, government, like business, waited out the storm. The idea that a depression might be a legitimate object for prevention or massive cure would have seemed not only impractical but in some way impious.

All this has changed in our times, beginning with the interventions against unemployment forced on every capitalist government during the Great Depression. And the change was not merely the gradual legitimation of the exercise of a wide variety of welfare functions, such as social security or income transfers to the poor. Much more ideologically difficult was the acceptance of the idea that the government could and should

43

take on responsibility for assuring a minimal level of economic performance. This was the meaning of the Keynesian "revolution" that seemed to nearly all businessmen at the time to be a doctrine of subversive intent and mischievous consequence.

The intent was certainly not subversive, Keynes being a person of profoundly conservative temperament, but the consequences were mischievous—although certainly less so than abandoning capitalism to the violent forces gathering within it at the time. For the effect of the growing size and scope of government policy has been to set the stage for an inflationary propensity where no such tendency had previously existed.

The linkage is both indirect as well as direct, complex and many sided. In part it is manifested simply in a change in public attitudes, a change that Daniel Yankelovich has called a growing "philosophy of entitlement." At all levels of society we have come to feel entitled not only to a higher level of economic security, but to an increase in our real incomes each year, regardless of whether we have personally increased our own measurable contribution to the system. Thus wages "automatically" rise, cost-of-living "escalators" are built into virtually all major wage and salary arrangments, and the pressure on costs relentlessly moves upward. That this is a consequence of government involvement cannot be unequivocally proved. But does anyone doubt that this upward drift of costs would quickly halt if government suddenly withdrew all responsibility for economic activity?

Another much more direct, although not necessarily more powerful, effect has been the addition of an enormous government-based demand to the demands generated by the private sector. Here we find not only the special, highly inflation-breeding demands of the military sector, with its indifference to competitive costs, but also the less visible demand generated by a growing proportion of the citizenry, mainly the old and the poor, whose spending is bolstered by government transfer payments. If we wanted to stop inflation dead in its tracks, we would only have to turn off the government spigot for arms and welfare, and in all likelihood the price level would begin to fall.

So would the economy as a whole, which is the reason why there is no possibility of such a massive disengagement from government. But the support provided by the government points to yet another source of its inflationary influence. The assumption of political responsibility for an acceptable level of economic performance pushes government—with only brief interludes—in the direction of an expansionary fiscal and monetary policy. Governments can withstand many setbacks, but not sustained recession. Thus the political pressure builds to spend high and tax low. In the United States in 1978 the federal deficit will probably top $60 billion, a ratio of deficit to gross national product that will be modest compared to

45

many European nations. Meanwhile, the rate of money creation continues to outpace the rate of growth of physical output. Output has been growing at about 2 to 3 percent a year over the last decade. Money supply has been growing between 6 to 10 percent a year, depending on how we define our it.

This does not mean that government spending in and of itself is a "cause" of inflation in a way that private spending is not. Who can tell whether the dollars in our pockets or bank accounts got there from some expenditure that originated in a firm or a public agency? If government spending is regarded as inflation generating, it is because the political motivation behind it has a stubborn inertia that contrasts with the more volatile spending behavior of the private sectors.

This problem of political motivation takes on particular importance if we examine another element in the changed institutional structure of capitalism. The inflationary capitalism of the last twenty years differs from preinflationary capitalism in the increased importance of large business enterprises teamed up with large unions. I say "teamed up" because a tacit conspiracy has been at work for the last decades, in which the central unions of the economy have won substantial wage increases from corporations which were quickly passed on (and in many cases more than passed on) through price increases.

This ganging up of big business and big labor against the public could not, however, have been carried out without the tacit complicity of the government which provided the "liquidity"—the sheer quantity of money available—needed to finance the larger payrolls and the larger consumer buying power. Had the Federal Reserve cracked down, the wage-price spiral would have come to a stop simply because corporations could not have financed wage increases and would have dug in their heels at the bargaining table. So the government again played a passive but powerful inflationary role in allowing private forces to exert their wills against the public. The reason the government did so, of course, was the enormous political opposition that it would have encountered (not to mention the economic damage it would have wrought) had it determined to keep the price lid on.

Inflation breeds crisis in social and political, as well as purely economic, ways. For the aspect of the inflationary process to which we ordinarily pay heed—the continuous rise in most prices—is only one side of a coin whose obverse is the continuous rise in nearly all incomes. When any price rises, someone must be receiving a larger payment. The difficulty presented by these rising incomes is that they are unevenly and "unfairly" distributed. In the inflationary spiral, one labor union, one industry, one region, one social stratum is always forging ahead of another. That is also the case, of course, in the absence of inflation, for technology or sheer bargaining power or the chance redistribution of buying power constantly favors some elements in the economy over others. But in the case of inflation, the act of gaining a march is highlighted and publicized. Fortunate or powerful companies, unions, or social groups are singled out for attention and blame. As a result, they serve as stimuli for redoubled efforts on the part of other groups that have been left behind.

Thus the uneven and uncoordinated pace of advance exacerbates a struggle for place that is always present within capitalist society. Every wage settlement, every major price announcement, every new tax or subsidy or welfare determination serves to mobilize the energies of other groups. Inflation in this way becomes self-perpetuating and self-aggravating, tending to convert the more or less settled pecking order of a stable social order into a Hobbesian struggle of each against all.

It is in large part because of this social melee that the inflationary process holds out the threat of getting beyond control. As the inflationary struggle becomes built into our everyday expectations, workers and capitalists alike seek to arrange their incomes in ways that will protect them from inflation. This leads to contracts with cost-of-living adjustments or other "indexing" arrangements designed to assure that everyone automatically stays even with the inflationary tide. Social Security recipients, for example, who would otherwise surely be losers in the inflationary race, are guaranteed against losses imposed by inflation through automatic adjustments in their checks as the cost-of-living index rises.

The consequence is that inflation becomes built into wage demands, materials contracts, and similar bargains because no one will sign a contract that penalizes him as prices rise. Worse, the rate of inflation tends to increase because everyone in the bargaining process seeks to come out ahead. In this way inflationary expectations engender inflation-producing actions, which in turn breed still higher inflationary expectations in a vicious and mounting spiral.

One of the most serious consequences of this universal anticipation of inflation affects the relationship of businesses to banks. In times of inflation it is always advantageous to be a borrower, because dollars will be more plentiful and cheaper when it comes time to repay the loan. Businesses therefore seek to borrow, but banks are loath to lend for exactly the same reasons. The consequences are twofold. First, interest rates go ever higher to compensate banks for the falling value of the dollars they will receive. Second, banks refuse to lend for more than short periods of time. The result is a piling up of short-term debt at very high interest rates. The high interest rates discourage businesses from pursuing their expansionary plans. And the piling up of large debts that must be continually renewed and repaid makes the banking system

Robert L. Heilbroner

extremely vulnerable to any untoward event— the failure of a large customer, the collapse of the market for real estate or commodities—that might impair its liquidity. The financial structure becomes overstrained and nervous. New York City approaches bankruptcy and the Chase Manhattan Bank holds its breath. The liquidity of the banking system—its ability to absorb a loss without resorting to panicky measures to gather cash—becomes a matter of general concern, rather than a matter taken for granted.

Added to these economic problems is a political one. For if the government is the main institutional cause and transmission agent for the new tendency toward inflation, it is also the main bulwark against a dangerous snowballing of the inflationary process. Thus, while governments create the conditions for inflation with one hand, they seek mightily to rein in the process with the other. Antiinflationary policies, including "credit crunches" (severe restrictions on the ability of banks to make loans), milder curtailments in the rate of growth of the money supply, budget cuts, admonitions and threats, buttons to be worn on lapels, have become familiar aspects of economic policy in all capitalist countries. None of them has been very effective. Therefore, they have all been accompanied, from time to time, by recourse to harsher measures—guidelines for wage and price increases, or outright wage and price controls, or deliberate policies to increase

50

unemployment as a "trade-off" against further price rises.

The trouble with the harsher measures is that they do not bring about a smooth deceleration of the inflationary process, but rather tend to tilt the economy from a boom path into a recession. Hurriedly, the repressive measures are then abandoned or reversed. As a result we have a pattern of "stop-go" business cycles made in Washington (or Whitehall or Bonn or Tokyo). Government itself thereby becomes a major source of economic instability and crisis as a direct consequence of trying to control the inflation for which its own presence and policies are in large measure responsible. This "contradiction" is political as much as economic, but it is as firmly set into the mechanism of modern-day capitalism as the older and simpler contradictions were rooted in the workings of the pre-statist economy.

VI

THE PRESENCE and destabilizing influence of inflation return us to an examination of the crisis through which we are now passing. For one central element in that crisis has still escaped our attention. This is the quixotic role played by the rise and subsequent fall of the American imperium.

We need not retrace here the history of that imperium, the child of the Cold War, of American ambitions and naiveté, of a vacuum left by the defeat of Germany and Japan and the exhaustion of England.

52

What interests us here are its economic consequences. Empires have always been expensive, and the American empire was no exception. In part the expense was military, requiring the establishment of a vast arms establishment at home and a network of bases abroad that underpinned the military capabilities of our client states, ranging from West Germany to Taiwan, from Spain to South Vietnam. The sheer military cost of this gigantic undertaking is beyond accurate calculation. For the United States alone it is roughly ten percent of our gross national product for the last 25 years (perhaps $2,000,000,000,000 in 1972 dollars), but that figure does not take into account the supplementary spending of other capitalist countries.

Of course this spending was justified at the time as a necessary countereffort to the imperialist expenditures of the Soviets (or the "Sino-Soviet bloc," as it was then called). No doubt there *was* a great deal of hostility and misperception on both sides, causing a mutual escalation of expenditures when a stabilization or even reduction might have been possible. But there seems little doubt, as Richard Barnet has recently argued in *The Giants,* that the United States took the lead in this dreadful contest of strengths. Primary, although not sole, responsibility for the trillions of dollars of military expenditures that have added their inflationary fuel to the world must be lodged with American imperial policy.

This was not, however, the only contribution of imperialism to inflation. The establishment of an American hegemony resulted not just in very large military expenditures, but in the rapid buildup of American capital investments abroad. Between 1950 and 1970, the value of American-owned plant and equipment abroad leaped from $12 billion to $78 billion. The necessity to pay for these assets, plus the need to pay for foreign military activity, culminating in the Vietnam War, resulted in a growing adverse balance of payments—that is, in a steadily mounting excess of payments that we made abroad, over and above payments made by foreigners to the United States. The items in the official register of international payments called "capital flows" began to register ominously persistent minus signs, as the net obligations of Americans to foreigners rose to a billion or two dollars per year by the mid 1950s, then to three and four billions per year by the mid 1960s, then to eight and nine billions in the early 1970s—erupting finally in a wild flow of $43 billion in 1976 (since then very considerably subsided).

The steady, apparently irreversible deterioration of the American balance of payments added international consequences to inflationary American imperial policy. For the external debts incurred by the United States had to be paid in one way or another. To some extent they were met by the shipment of American gold to foreign nations to whom we owed dollars. Between 1949 and 1970 we sold about $14 billion of our gold hoard—more than half of it—to meet foreign claims.

But the major portion was not paid in gold. We didn't have that much gold. It was paid by persuading foreign creditors to allow their bills to remain unpaid, piling up as IOUs in the form of dollar balances in American banks. A dollar in an American bank may not seem like an IOU, but we made it one by asking the foreign owners of these dollars not to exercise their legal right to convert these dollars into gold. If they wanted to spend their balances for American goods, fine. If they wanted to repatriate them as gold, not so fine.

Only an imperial nation can impose such conditions on its creditors, and it does so not by outright coercion, but simply by persuading them that there is no alternative to accepting the imperial currency, lest the entire financial structure come tumbling down. Until very recently the foreign banks and bankers of the world understood and accepted this fact. As the American balance of payments continued to register its negative balances, the holdings of dollar balances by foreign banks rose precipitously, from about $12 billion in the mid 1960s to $113 billion in late 1977. If we included the dollar holdings of multinational corporations, there were estimated to be $400 billion in foreign hands.

The steady piling up of dollar IOUs came as no pleasure to foreign governments. For these American dollar balances served as new reserves for their banks, encouraging them to expand their lending and investing operations. It was impossible to "sterilize" an addition to bank reserves that exceeded $100 billion, taking dollars and gold together. Thus the chronic adverse balance of payments in the United States resulted in an immense increase in the supply of European and Japanese banking reserves. In turn that resulted in a surge of inflation abroad, where prices rose, as we have noted, much more steeply than at home.

None of this could have happened had not the American imperial presence been deemed of such critical importance. To preserve the peace and security of the capitalist world was an American ambition that no European nation wanted to undo. But the price of acquiescence in American power was a willingness to permit the United States to incur an "unlimited" deficit in its balance of payments by forcing its creditors to accept IOUs, rather than gold, as payment for the net goods and services and assets bought by Americans. As these IOUs, in the form of balances in American banks, became part of the other nations' money supplies, America's creditors watched with helpless dismay as the costs of empire were transferred to them in the form of an inescapable inflation.

In all likelihood, an inflationary tendency would have disturbed the postwar world, whatever the American role, for the growth in government responsibility and expenditure was much more advanced in most of Europe than in the United States. But the advent of the American hegemony vastly magnified the problem. During the period of uncontested American world power—roughly up to the turning point of the Vietnam War—so immense was the flow of spending for military purposes overseas, so rapid the buildup of the American-owned foreign assets, and so powerful the American influence over the financial policies of its client states, that the mere operation of the American imperium by itself was in all likelihood a sufficient condition for the globalization of the inflationary phenomenon.

The crisis that began in the early 1970s reflects the collapse of that imperium equally as much as it reflects the more dramatic single event of oil shock. Just as the unchallenged primacy of American economic strength gave rise to a continual piling up of dollar balances, so the gradual decline of that strength removed the inhibitions that prevented foreign governments or speculators from considering any currency as preferable to the dollar. And the erosion of American power was already increasingly evident and worrisome from the middle 1960s. Long before the Vietnam debacle, it was clear that American arms could not prevent the rise of revolutionary governments in the underdeveloped world. Starting in the mid 1960s, the American international balance on merchandise account—the net surplus of our exports of goods and services over our imports—began to show an alarming fall, indicating that the day of uncontested American domination in key markets was rapidly coming to an end—worse, that America was a much more "exposed" economy than had been assumed. Not least, perhaps, the outbreak of race riots and student unrest showed the world that the United States was not immune from the internal troubles that were evident in other capitalist states.

One never knows how skepticism turns into disbelief, much less into overt action. Thus a world that was studiously trying to ignore the changing balance of real power was taken by surprise when the London gold market suddenly ran amok in March 1968. Prior to that time the market had normally sold about 3 to 4 tons of gold per day. Then on March 1 a surge of demand for gold led to the sale of 40 tons. By March 14 the daily sales were 200 tons. Almost exclusively these sales represented conversions of privately held dollars into bullion. By mid-March the United States Treasury was being forced to put $1 million worth of gold into the market every two or three minutes to satisfy demand, a rate of supply that would have exhausted the nation's entire stock of gold in about two weeks.

After a frantic weekend conference in Washington, the hemorrhage was staunched by an agreement not to sell gold on the London market to private bidders. The new arrangement lasted a short while, as governments

—fearing that a collapse of the dollars would undermine the safety of their *own* currencies—agreed to go on accepting dollars without trying to convert them into gold. The United States, on its side, agreed to bring its unruly balance of payments into order, so that it would stop creating the deficits that were forcing dollars on unwilling holders.

The pledges were in vain—the U.S. balance of payments steadily worsened as our imports soared and our exports failed to follow suit. Another assault on the dollar followed, and another international effort to prop it up. Finally, in 1973, the pressures became too great to allow the existing "fixed" relationship of dollars to other currencies to continue. With grave misgivings, the dollar was officially severed from gold, making it impossible for America's creditors to change their balances into bullion; and the dollar was allowed to "float" at whatever prices supply and demand dictated for it.

The results at first were not too bad. Despite the gigantic holdings of dollars by foreigners, nothing like a panic developed. As travelers to Europe soon discovered, the dollar fell ten or twenty percent. French francs that used to be reckoned as "worth" 20 cents were thought of as quarters; Swiss francs that used to be quarters became worth 35 or 40 cents. The fact that nervous individuals around the world were buying gold, which rose nearly to $200 an ounce, indicated that some people distrusted *all* paper currencies, but aside from that manifestation of anxiety or psychosis, calm prevailed in the world of international finance.

We do not know what finally upset this tense but essentially inactive state of affairs. For whatever reason, in 1977 the sentiment of the international financial community—the banks, the multinationals, the owners of private bank accounts here and abroad—again turned decisively against the United States. Foreign holders of American balances now wanted marks, yen, francs (especially Swiss francs), rials, krone, not because they necessarily "believed" in those currencies, but because they sought the only hedge against the risks of financial life—diversification. Thus they sold their dollars right and left, and the dollar descended to the lowest level in modern history. With the descent came the fear of a caving-in of large financial networks. A fall in a basic currency always brings such risks. If an American company owing sums abroad cannot meet its obligations (which are now dearer), it may fail. If it fails, a local bank where it may be a very large depositor may also fail. If the local bank fails, a great central city bank may fail. If a great central city bank fails, depositors across the nation may try to convert their deposits into cash. So the nightmare goes.

One never knows when such fantasies might become actualities. Perhaps another flight from the dollar will yet bring down the financial structure that holds together the capitalist mechanism. But it seems unlikely. The United States economy is still the most powerful in the world; and if its position as a manufacturer is now less secure, its position as supplier of food to the world was never more important. Unlike France, Italy, or England, it faces no opposition party whose policies would force large-scale adaptations of the system or an attempted conversion to "socialism." The American recession, costly though it has been, has not produced serious political or social unrest. We have been mercifully spared European terrorism. American inflation is still below that of most of the rest of the industrial world, and the prices of shares on its stock exchanges are, by comparative standards, cheap. Thus, by all the criteria of history or common sense, the dollar would seem to be one of the soundest, not one of the frailest, currencies.

Obviously something is missing from this calculus. It is almost surely an element that cannot be "factored in" according to some reasonable formula. Searching for the nature of this irrational conviction—a conviction that has led the world's capitalist financiers and investors to reject the currency of the capitalist nation that has thus far survived the twentieth century with the least damage to its political, social, and economic structure—I am led to conjecture that it may be precisely its good fortune that makes America the present target of forward-looking speculative opinion. "You are yet to be tested," declares the rest of the world;

"You have yet to run the gauntlet." From such a perspective the dollar becomes a currency to avoid, not because it is imperiled today but because it may become imperiled tomorrow, when the crisis reaches American shores in full force.

But, of course, the act of getting out of a currency today in anticipation of tomorrow causes it to fall now, not later. The recent currency convulsion was thus a vivid example of just such a self-fulfilling prophecy—assuming, of course, that what lay behind it were the kinds of expectations I have raised, and not some profound structural defect in the American economy that escaped domestic eyes but was visible abroad.

Meanwhile, the battering of the dollar, with its message of a loss of faith in the American economy among those who would be expected to be its strongest supporters, created a pall of near Stygian gloom on Wall Street. In April 1978, "depression" was not the word to describe the condition of the economy, but it was assuredly appropriate to Wall Street's state of mind. A respected investment counselor of long acquaintance, who has been a consistent voice of moderate optimism during the last years, confessed to me over lunch one day early that month that he had finally surrendered to the prevailing opinion. "I don't know what lies behind the black mood of the Street," he said, "but I have finally come to share it. Have you read *The Crash of '79?* Not the nuclear part, but the complete breakdown, the wild inflation, that sort of thing? It's absurd,

62

but that's the talk you hear these days. I won't add to
that talk, but I don't think you can buck it."

About ten days later the stock market roared up one
Friday with over 50 million shares changing hands—
the largest volume ever—and then broke *that* record
the following Monday. Why? The talk on the Street
was: "All the bad news is now behind us." Or: "The
Arabs are finally hungry." Or: "It was long overdue."
Such is the quality of deep analysis by which the Street
explains itself to itself. At any rate, for the moment, the
crise was over. The underlying crisis, as we shall see,
was not.

VII

WHAT BROUGHT ABOUT this *crise* in the first place? The psychological history of capitalism is a tale of alternating euphoria and despair. We tend to think of the late nineteenth century as a period of huge self-confidence and ebullience, but the diaries of the captains of industry reveal another mood just below the surface, a mood described by economic historian E. C. Kirkland as "panic and pain." When recessions struck with their never-quite-predictable regularity, the latent mood surfaced, and businessmen

64

tore their collars and feared for the end. "All the fortune I have made has not served to compensate for the anxiety of that period," wrote John D. Rockefeller, looking back on forty years of a career that we think of as an unbroken series of triumphs.

The labile business state of mind was no doubt the consequence in the first place of the continual buffeting to which business was subject. But I suspect there was another reason as well. It was—and is—that capitalism never found a rationale that entirely dispelled the anxieties of the business world as to the viability of the capitalist mechanism, again and again teetering at the edge of what seemed like collapse; nor did capitalism ever gain a credo that rescued it, once for all, from the doubts and criticisms of its moral critics. The economics profession, writing at an Olympian level of abstraction after the 1870s, and concerning itself more and more with problems of "equilibrium" and "pure competition" that had no visible counterpart in the real world, could not convince businessmen that the rocking economic system was an unsinkable ship with a foolproof self-righting mechanism. And the moralists of the system (many of them also economists) never quite explained away the tendency of the system to create poverty alongside riches and squalor along with success. Here the problem was that the culture that produced the economic values embodied in a capitalist system also produced the political and social values embodied in a bourgeois democracy. Thus, unlike previous economic systems, capitalism has always been exposed to an egalitarian countercurrent that undermined the simple endorsement of inequality characteristic of precapitalist societies.

As a result, the state of mind of the capitalist class has always been insecure and defensive during a crisis—insecure because it was never entirely convinced that the economic vehicle would not tip over, defensive because it could never entirely square the results of the economic system with the values of its social and political beliefs. It is interesting, from this point of view, to reflect on the number of businessmen (and the even greater number of their widows) who turned into reformers of one kind or another, usually trying to temper the raw workings of the marketplace to bring its results into closer consonance with their moral beliefs. What other system has produced such a show of uneasy conscience?

It is, I think, this uneasy conscience, quite as much as the unsettled questions regarding the stability of the system, that accounts for the swings in mood that have always assailed the system. For periods of crisis not only test the operational capabilities of the system, but also the ultimate granite on which it rests—the loyalty, or at least the acquiescence, of the labor force on which it depends. The cooperation of that labor force is no longer won, as it was in Marx's time, by a reliance on the lash of sheer need, or by the limitation of its suffrage, or the steadying hand of venerable traditions of the natural superiority of the rich. The cooperation of the work force today is secured by the systematic misrepresentation of the system as a kind of large, hearty, and cheerful family. Corporations that command immense wealth and make strategic decisions of global importance portray themselves as "just folks," personified by the ordinary people who are featured in their institutional advertisements. Consciously or otherwise, the media present an image of the capitalist world as a great cornucopia of commodities available to all, where laughing young women and energetic young men make their serious, playful determinations as to what car to buy, soap to use, bank to borrow from. The "problems" of the system are presented as detached from, and in no way connected with, its "successes." The central facts of the system are ignored so that it becomes almost a radical statement when Paul Samuelson writes in his famous text that a pyramid of personal incomes in the United States, constructed with children's blocks each representing $1000, would soar far higher than the Eiffel Tower, although most of the population would be within an yard of the ground.

A vast hypocrisy is thus characteristic of the self-advertisement of capitalism, a hypocrisy that threatens the system in moments of crisis because there is always the risk that it will be recognized for what it is, with who knows what consequences. Thus when confidence wanes, it is not only because the omnipresent danger of a collapse is again experienced, but because the

Robert L. Heilbroner

social and political legitimacy of the system must again be put to the test. I suspect that all capitalist nations experience this unease because of the inescapable conflict between their extreme economic privileges and their social and political egalitarian tendencies and commitments, but perhaps in America this tension is greatest and the ensuing insecurity most keenly felt.

I raise these speculative considerations because one must search for some explanation of the black mood that haunted the financial and business world in late 1977 and early 1978. As with the international economic picture, one could not explain the heavy tone of the stock market, that traditional barometer of confidence, merely in terms of a calculus based on realistic projections. When the stocks that made up the Dow Jones Average could be bought for an aggregate price that was less than their book value, the market was predicting some terrible occurence. What could that occurence have been? A minor dip in the rate of economic growth—the worst that anyone expected for the next year or so? An increase in the rate of inflation by a percentage point, or even by two percentage points? A failure to write a stringent energy bill—or perhaps the opposite, the achievement of such a bill? None of these and similar eventualities, endlessly discussed in the business pages, warranted the kind of determined pessimism that Wall Street showed, a pessimism that converted even such stalwart optimists as my investment counselor friend.

The answer must have been, I believe, that The Street was predicting something far more serious. It was predicting that behind behind the manifest not-too-serious crisis lurked the possibility of a profound, even catastrophic crisis, a crisis from which the system could not recover, at least in anything like its present shape. As with the international financial world, the domestic financial community was weighing the future of the system in its mind. The crisis was not not one of present realities but of expected developments, not one of economics alone but of belief.

VIII

IN ORDER TO UNDERSTAND that ominous prognosis, we must examine one last aspect of capitalist crisis. This is its positive, or better, curative, function.

For crisis can, and usually does, play a constructive role, even though it brings blockage and disruption. Conservatives have always stressed this role, speaking of the "purgative" benefits of a recession, a diagnosis that sounds heartless insofar as it pays no heed to the suffering that the purgative imposes, but which

70

nonetheless accurately describes the potential effects of the medicine on the patient, who is the system and not its individual participants.

The curative purposes served by a crisis are not difficult to identify if we simply review the characteristic features of a recession. Production falls or growth is slowed. Unemployment increases. The stock market is depressed or may have a "crash." Bankruptcies rise. Sellers' markets become buyers' markets, as power shifts from those who command labor or materials to those who command money.

All these effects putatively combine to yield one major consequence. They tend to restore the conditions that permit the great circuit of accumulation to resume its normal operation. Labor or raw materials markets that were too tight become slack once more. Discipline becomes easier to maintain on the factory floor because of the rising threat of unemployment and the increasing pressures on factory managers. Glutted markets eventually absorb excess goods, and demand picks up as buyers reorder for inventory and replacement. The sorry state of business lessens the demand for bank credit, and the banks gradually regain their liquidity. Government welfare measures continue to pump out money but its tax structure takes in less money, so that aggregate buying is supported by what economists call the "automatic stabilizers."

These curative effects depend on a fluid economy that responds in appropriate fashion to the bitter medicine administered to it. The same medicine, given to an economy that suffers from an advanced state of organizational rigidity, may not cure the crisis or restore vigor. The ecomony may simply continue in a depressed condition more or less indefinitely. Behind the Keynesian diagnosis of the possibility of an equilibrium at less than full employment was the tacit recognition that a mature capitalism could not undergo the "loosening up" that a crisis requires to work its effects. Then we have continuing doses of medicine without resuscitative effect—the "stagflation" of recent years.

Yet, speaking historically, there is no doubt that crises remove the obstacles that block the accumulative process. Out of crises, with their social misery—in part, out of that misery itself—have come the conditions for a new period of growth and expansion.

Crises and their sequelae are not *just* curative episodes, however. As Marx was the first to point out, not only does the capitalist system unfold through a more or less regular succession of booms and crises, but the crises themselves exert lasting and cumulative effects on the system. The business cycle, in other words, is not just a wavelike movement of production, but a movement of the whole socioeconomic order through history; and the measure of the cycle therefore requires that we pay heed not alone to its quantitative effects on production or prices or employment, but also to its qualitative impact on the organization of the society itself.

Two such changes seemed to Marx of central importance. One was the tendency of repeated crises to bring into being an economy of giant enterprises. Each crisis encouraged the formation of large enterprises because smaller and weaker firms were the typical victims of economic hesitations and downturns, while stronger and larger firms survived to buy up and integrate the assets of their competitors. "Capital grows to a huge mass in a single hand in one place," Marx wrote in *Capital,* "because it has been lost by many in another place." This process, which was only in its incipient stage in Marx's time, has changed the world of "competitive capitalism" of the 1860s into that of the "monopoly capitalism" of the present day.

At a deeper level the effect is even more dramatic, and certainly more important, than the rise of large-scale production. Enormous enterprises require extensive internal planning, as John Kenneth Galbraith has repeatedly pointed out. At the same time, the rise of a vast, integrated core of industrial firms—the five hundred largest of which produce a value of output almost as big as that of the remaining 400,000-odd industrial enterprises—brings into being a structural organization of capitalism that differs very little in technology or organization from that of the ministries of a socialist economy. Thus, while capitalism clings tenaciously to its beliefs in the "privateness" of property, it has in fact created an economic milieu in which property has become ever more social. This unintended socialization of the productive forces of the system was felt by Marx to be the "contradiction" that above all else directed the long-term development of capitalism toward socialism.

A second textural change envisaged by Marx affected the social rather than the technological or organizational aspects of capitalism. He saw the hammer blows of successive crises altering the class structure of the system in ways that he also felt to be ultimately incompatible with the legal privileges of a capitalist order. One of these alterations—again stunningly confirmed by history—was the elimination of petty proprietorships and independent artisanships as dominant forms of social being. The competitive powers of capitalist production, he felt, were unchallengeable by the small producer. All would be forced eventually to become sellers of their wage-labor—proletarians— rather than sellers of their own products.

The prediction is again fully confirmed by events. In the early 1800s, for example, about four-fifths of all American working people were self-employed as farmers, artisans, small businessmen, and the like. Only about ten percent of the labor force is self-employed today, and one-third of the labor force works for the central core of the great Five Hundred Firms.

The political consequences of this "proletarianization" of capitalism have not, however, accorded with Marx's general expectations. Although more and more of the work force has become drawn into the capital-wage relationship, the newly created proletarians have not developed a unitary class consciousness nor experienced a welling up of revolutionary will. Instead, a process of "bourgeoisification," already foreseen and lamented by Engels, has forestalled the militancy and insurgency on which the revolutionary prognosis ultimately hinged. Veblen, perhaps more clearly than Marx, anticipated the consequences of a system of high productive powers and democratic views: The lower orders would look to the upper classes as models to be aped, not as masters to be dethroned. Thus the hypocritical and biased self-advertisement of capitalism has been received not with skepticism but faith, embraced by a working class that wanted to believe in the benign workings and accessible heights of the business world.

Only recently have we had disturbing evidences of a turning away from the system, most dramatically played out in the terrorist tactics of European revolutionary gangs, but perhaps more significantly manifested in the anticapitalist mood of student bodies throughout the world. No one knows, of course, whether these movements will become full-fledged threats to the stability of the system. That depends, probably, on whether the working class can be won from its conservative views to a "genuinely" proletarian perspective. Although that has not yet

Robert L. Heilbroner

been the case in any capitalist nation, the advent of a crisis always raises the spectre of such a revolutionary "awakening." Thus crisis comes not only as a test to the working order of the economy, but also to the reliability of its moral order and its traditional observances and obeisances. It is this test, I think, that troubles the sleep of the guardians of the system today far more than the economic damage that has been suffered or that seems likely to come.

Thus crisis spells cumulative change, not just advance and retreat. Moreover, at crucial junctures, crisis seems to usher in changes of seismic magnitude, changes that alter the very institutional underpinnings of the system. In the view of David Gordon, a leading young American Marxist scholar, some crises are fulcral points in the historical unfolding of capitalism, bringing structural adjustments that are necessary in order to allow the clogged circuit of production to open again. These crucial turning points are, Gordon suggests, coincident with—indeed, the very basis of—the rather mysterious fifty year cycles, dimly visible like ghosts in the scanty and fragmentary statistics of nineteenth and early twentieth century production and prices, and discovered by the Soviet economist N. D. Kondratief. (He was later liquidated by Stalin.)

Whatever the role or reality of the Kondratief cycle, there is no doubt that some crises are more significant than others, because they seem to produce relatively swift and far-reaching alterations in the structure of the

76

system. In Gordon's view, for example, the crisis of 1848 opened the way for an era of mechanization that was to provide the momentum of the period up to the turn of the century. The crisis of 1893 touched off a "crystallization" of the structure of industrial markets, as the pent-up forces of technology and organization found a workable organizational form in the merger movement that opened the way for the rise of Big Business Prosperity until the crash of 1929. And the crisis of 1929 ushered in a complex transformation whose major institutional change was the expansion of the public sector and the deliberate use of government spending as a supplement to private demand.

No doubt it is possible to argue with many aspects of this large-scale effort at historical explanation. But Gordon's suggestion that we search for important institutional shifts at critical points in the history of capitalism strikes me as very fruitful. In particular, the hypothesis suggests that we may today be located at such an inflection point, and that the crisis of our period, whether it be marked by a stock market crash or boom in '79, may be most clearly understood in terms of the institutional shifts it requires and will probably bring about.

The immediate cause of that crisis, we have said, can be traced to the worldwide impact of the oil embargo that quadrupled energy prices within a year. But we know that oil shock was only the precipitating factor in a situation that was already highly crisis-prone. The

American hegemony and the arms expenditures that supported it gave impetus to a worldwide inflationary momentum that further increased the potential for economic disruption. Prior to that, the enormous swelling of the public sector within the economies of all capitalist nations had itself created the conditions for eventual instability, partly by giving rise to inflation, partly by creating unsustainable expectations of social entitlement. And anterior even to that, by the late 1960s there were many signs of older forms of crisis-proneness—a tightening of labor markets, a mounting indiscipline in the labor process, a growing satiation in important markets.

The normal curative results of a crisis can be expected to dissolve some of these blockages. The enormous overhang of unwanted dollars will gradually move into stronger hands and some of the dollar deficit will become extinguished by being bought by Americans. The stock market has already regained its aplomb and has decided that the prospects for the Ford Motor Company, to take an instance, warrant paying a price of more than three times its earnings for its shares—the price-earnings ratio in early '78. Even inflation, the most continuously anxiety producing of all the forces making for crisis, may well be partially cured by the recession. Between 1976 and the first quarter of 1978, the inflation rate has been substantially reduced in most European countries (in England it was almost cut in half). Moreover, as the recession holds back the pace of advance, "surplusses" of oil appear and cause prices to weaken, as has already happened on the West Coast. Thus as so often before, the bitter medicine of recession can be expected to exert its purgative effects, clearing away some of the obstacles to capital accumulation, and permitting some resumption of the momentum pent up in a million profit-seeking entrepreneurs.

Yet I do not think that these normal absorptive processes will, by themselves, suffice to get the system back to the steady and sustained growth of the 1950s and 1960s. For reasons that we shall see, perhaps such a full-scale resumption of the longest boom in capitalist history will be impossible in any event. But I think it is likely that deep changes will be required to restore sustained, if more modest, growth to the system. To come directly to the point, I believe they will take the completion of an institutional shift that is already begun, although like all such shifts, much misunderstood and resisted. The shift is to economic planning, the only institutional transformation that can, in my opinion, give a new measure of life, albeit a limited one, to the capitalist system.

IX

To JUSTIFY AN ARGUMENT for so drastic a change in institutional arrangements, we must be able to discover some element in the present crisis that is quantitatively large enough and qualitatively different enough to warrant another major restructuring of the capitalist framework. I suggest there is such an element in the challenges posed to the process of capitalist accumulation by what we loosely call "the environment"—the complex and intercon-

80

nected constraints of our energy supplies, our resource availabilities, our pollution dangers.

The problems of the environment are now so generally familiar that I shall not try to marshall the standard facts and figures. Let us instead consider the ways in which some of these constraints impinge on the capitalist process. Here we might begin again with oil shock, which has already dealt the system a serious, although certainly not fatal, blow. But present-day oil shock is not the full measure of the problem. Today's oil prices are artificially maintained by the coordinated action of the OPEC cartel, not by the pressure of demand against supply. Meanwhile, demand is steadily increasing and the day will come when it is the pull of demand, and not the prop of a cartel agreement, that sets the price of oil. Moreover, the difference between the most optimistic and pessimistic dates as to that "crossover" point—optimistic dates assuming a high rate of new oil discoveries and effective conservation plans, and pessimistic dates assuming the converse—is surprisingly small. In both cases, crossover occurs during the next twenty years. Thereafter demand will be in charge and we can expect the price of oil to rise steadily, with no help from OPEC at all, unless we find substitutes for gasoline and heating oil.

The coming rise of oil prices is only the leading edge of a series of such changes that will affect the very possibility of economic growth, interfering with the first phase of capital accumulation in a hitherto unknown way. The stringency of worldwide resources, while not imposing anything like an oil bottleneck, will nonetheless be sufficiently great during the coming years of this century to necessitate vast investments in mineral extraction and food production. According to a study of global needs conducted for the U.N. by Nobel Laureate Wassily Leontief, the consumption of common minerals must rise fivefold, food fourfold, if a moderate rate of global growth is to continue. These requirements will necessitate stupendous economic, and no less stupendous social and political, commitments.

And then, of course, the fragility of the atmospheric and liquid mantle pose the last and perhaps most formidable obstacle of all. Human activity, especially in the industrial regions where its effect on nature is most concentrated, is at the verge of creating violent and irreversible effects on the planet. Nothing is more sobering in this connection than the recent scientific debate as to whether fluorocarbons—the propellant gas in hairsprays and underarm deodorants—posed a serious threat to the filtrating properties of the atmosphere. What was sobering was not the outcome of the debate—the consensus was that the danger was not clear and immediate—but the tacitly accepted premise that the volume of these gaseous releases was so large that it might actually endanger human health. The same immense scale of technological assult on the environment is indicated by the ongoing debates over the possibility of carbon dioxide creating a "greenhouse effect" that would alter the temperature of the earth, or the possibility that massed industrial heat could change the patterns of air circulation and rain precipitation, or that the release of chemical waste could contaminate ground water, or that the volume of nuclear wastes would constitute a massive hazard.

All these new realities point in the same direction. They indicate the need for an unprecedented degree of monitoring, control, supervision, and precaution over the economic process. Some of these safeguarding functions can perhaps be performed by the marketplace itself, particularly insofar as the allocation of scarce resources is concerned. But the market will not monitor safety, nor will it impose decisions about the rate of growth, or its sharing within or among countries, that accord with the moral and political, as well as the economic, desires of peoples and nations. Thus the constraints of our time, the need for which will steadily intensify as far ahead as we can see, imply a powerful, and I think irresistible, force for planning the economic process in a way that has never before been necessary.

What is new about the thrust toward planning is its purpose. Some aspects of planning are by now familiar. We plan to develop appropriate transportation networks, whether road or rail or air. We plan to develop rural, or now urban, hinterlands. We plan to carry on the fiscal and monetary and welfare functions on which economic life depends. To be against planning, as such, is to be for chaos, not for laissez-faire.

But the planning that will emerge from the present crisis will be of a different nature. Its essential purpose will not be to remedy the various failures that capitalist growth has brought, but to direct, and at bottom to protect, the very possibility of such growth, as long as that can be. This will certainly require the formulation of strict policies with respect to the use of energy. It must embrace an ever wider range of considerations affecting the environment. The process of scientific development and technological application must likewise fall more and more under the guidance and, where necessary, the veto power of government.

All this will involve allocations of materials, prohibitions against certain kinds of investment or consumption activities, and a general sticking of the public nose into private life, wherever that life, left to itself, threatens the long-term viability of the system.

This sort of planning seems an inescapable direction in which capitalism must move if its work of accumulation is to proceed as long as possible without encroaching suicidally on the carrying capacity of the planet. But the fact that the purpose of national planning will be to assist the continued functioning of the system does not mean that it will be welcomed by the business community, perhaps with the exception of a small advance guard that always sees further than the pack. On the contrary, the steady intermeshing of state and economy will be feared and fought as tantamount to a surrender to socialism. Indeed, that fear and that fight *are* the current crisis, quite as much as the actual blockage of circuits by oil or inflation. It is the vision of an impending "socialism" as one outcome of the present trend, alternating with even more alarming visions of an end to the acceptance of the morality and legitimacy of the system, that account, I think, for the dark and nameless fears that beset the capitalist world in general.

As I have already said, one cannot predict whether the legitimacy of the system will in fact be shaken. There are some reasons for thinking not: the failure of the Left to gain its expected victories in Europe, the repeated disappointments and disillusions about the economic and political performance of the communist nations, and perhaps most of all the absence of a plausible program for a socialist restructuring of society that would "make a difference." But there are reasons as well for disquiet: the apparently irresistible decline in public standards of behavior, the disappearance of the economic patriotism that sustained our parents, the loss of sophisticated belief in the appeal of capitalism. The existing governments of Europe do not govern in the name of capitalism but in the name of order; and it is order itself that has become the enemy of youth.

Thus we shall live for a long period, in all likelihood, in the shadow of a crisis of faith. However unforeseeable the outcome of that trial, I think one can predict with a fair degree of assurance that the institutional changes necessary for national planning will come, despite the vociferous opposition that they will raise.

In fact, the skeleton of such a planning effort already exists in the scatter of agencies and authorities and Departments of our government, and in more formally designated Planning Commissions and Boards in the majority of other capitalist nations. It would be foolish to believe that these agencies and authorities will "solve" the problem of assuring a smooth continuation of capitalist growth, any more than the rise of welfare agencies or Keynesian economics solved the problems of poverty or unemployment. Yet Social Security and unemployment insurance and the deliberate managment of the economy did protect a highly vulnerable system against a threat that might well have ruptured its accumulation circuit for good. In the same way, we can anticipate that the new planning effort, despite its inevitable mistakes, inefficiencies, wastes, and aggravations, will prevent a similar interruption, of perhaps even greater dimensions, from bringing the system to a halt.

X

AND IN THE END? No doubt there will be still another deep crisis. Moreover, it may come more rapidly, for the pace of change seems to be quickening. Branco Horvat, a widely known Yugoslavian economist, has pointed out that the era of competitive capitalism lasted 175 years, from roughly 1700 to 1875; the era of monopoly capitalism, 55 years, from 1875 to 1930; welfare capitalism, 43 years, from 1930 to 1973. Assuming that I am right, and that we are now entering the era of planned capitalism, how long will it last?

That is a question to which we can give only the most tentative answers. The constraints of the environment, which are the great determining element in the era into which we are moving, suggest that we have perhaps 25 years of growth (as the Leontief study also suggests), followed thereafter by an almost certain drastic curtailment. But meanwhile there are other contradictions and barriers and hindrances that may induce a crisis before we reach that winding down of expansion which, by its very definition, would impose a truly historic challenge to capitalism. There is, for example, the suffocating growth of bureaucracy, itself the by-product of the welfare state and the planned state—another "contradiction," if you will. There is the rampant expansion of industrial technology, bringing not only the ever-greater socialization of the economic structure but what seems to be a concomitant disaffection, indifference, and antipathy of a population unable to find satisfaction in the plastic wealth or the impersonal employments that industrialism generates. There is the lingering, always explosive problem of the distribution of wealth, justice, and decency within the rich nations, and between the rich nations and the poor ones. There is the unsettled state of the economic world, with capitalist nations hesitating between live-and-let-live and beggar-my-neighbor philosophies; and developed nations and undeveloped ones eyeing one another in mixed need and hatred. And there are violence and despair and the slow erosion of order-maintaining behavior. Any of these may become the entering wedge of a new crisis, pushing for further adaptations that may ultimately exceed the capabilities of the system.

But this is still some distance into the future, I think. History has shown capitalism to be an extraordinarily resilient, persisting, and tenacious system, perhaps because its driving force is dispersed among so much of its population rather than concentrated solely in a governing elite. In pursuit of the privileges, the beliefs, above all the profits of capitalism, its main protagonists have not only created the material wonders that Marx marveled at, but shown a capacity for changefulness that even he, who never underestimated the self-preserving drive of capital, did not fully anticipate. Thus it is still too soon to write finis to the present era, for in our time capitalism has yet another subchapter within its power to create, and perhaps others after that. But already we can see more clearly than past generations that the chapter cannot go on forever, and that in our own time we will have to live through periods of wrenching change even if the system survives. What comes thereafter is still a closed book.

Notes and Comments

I

The Crash of '79 is by Paul Erdman, Simon and Schuster, New York, 1976.

II

The analysis of capitalist growth through three inter-connected phases follows very loosely the schema laid out by Marx in *Capital,* Volume 2, Chapters 1–4. Anyone familiar with those chapters will see that I have made no effort to reproduce the analysis with exactitude. I use the "three phases approach" partly because it seems to me readily comprehensible to someone who has not been exposed to conventional analysis, and partly because it is much more suggestive with regard to the origin of crises than the diagram by which the economy is represented in most texts. This conventional diagram is a great wheel in which "households" and "businesses" are connected by arrows showing money payments moving in one direction, and goods and services in the other. (In addition, there is often a "loop" in the diagram showing how savings must filter through the banks to reappear as investment, to keep the circular flow moving.) That conventional representation is useful for some purposes, mainly to establish the self-renewing nature of the economic process, but it is at too high a level of abstraction to be useful as an entrée to systemic failure.

III

There is an interesting issue concealed in this discussion of the three stages. In Marx's formulation, profits were generated solely in the second stage, where labor power, put to use, yielded up the "surplus value" that accrued to the employer. Conventional economists

(and perhaps some contemporary Marxists) would locate the source of profit in the first phase, where employers may buy materials and equipment or labor
below their true values, or in the third phase, where
capitalists may sell products at "monopoly" prices,
above their true values. Many theoretical consequences follow from the "location" of profits, but they
do not affect the fundamental dynamics of the system
that we are examining here.

IV

When Marx presents the panorama of capitalist reproduction and growth, he lays special emphasis on a
unique problem that he discovered in its midst. We can
divide all production into two "sectors," or "departments," as Marx called them: a flow of consumer
goods and a flow of investment goods. In each of these
"departments" there is an *internal* demand for the output of the department concerned. That is, the workers
and capitalists of the consumer goods department will
themselves buy consumer goods; and the capitalists of
the investment goods department will themselves buy
investment goods (machines to replace their worn-out
equipment). Thus part of total output of the economy
will be disposed of within the respective departments
that produce it.

But part will not. For the value of the consumer

output includes not only the wages and profits that will be spent on consumption goods and services, but also the costs of the wear and tear that must be spent for the replacement of machinery, and not for consumption goods. Similarly, in the investment department, the part of the value of output represented by the cost of depreciation will be spent to buy machines to replace those used up by this department; but the costs of output attributable to wages and profits will not be spent for machinery, but will go instead for consumption goods.

Therefore, an exchange must take place, and a flow of "excess" goods from the investment goods sector must be sold to the consumption goods sector, in exchange for a flow of "excess" consumer goods that will go from the consumption department to the investment department. Marx's pioneering identification of this necessary "fit" in a self-reproducing economy presages work that has since blossomed into Wassily Leontief's input-output analysis, perhaps the most important practical achievement in economics of the century.

Marx's analysis differs in one way, however, from that of present economic analysis. Contemporary economists would agree that there must be a "matching" of outputs between sectors, as well as between individual producers and the demands for particular items. To Marx, this challenge of matching was left more or less unanalyzed. To put it differently, the challenge of establishing matches was seen by him only as an illustration of the pervasive "anarchy," or planlessness, of the capitalist mechanism, and therefore as an endemic source of crises for it.

Contemporary non-Marxist economists stress an aspect of the system passed over by Marx, namely the "signals" that the marketplace itself generates, when matches do not occur. When, for example, there are too many (or too few) machines offered to the consumption goods sector, the resulting fall (or rise) of machine prices "tells" the machine-making capitalists whether production should be increased or diminished. In this way, conventional economics sees the system as moving gradually toward a "fit." The Marxian reply would stress the time required to make these adjustments, and the likelihood that further mismatches would take place while the adjustment process was under way. Whether or not we use the terminology of Marx, this confidence in the ability of the system to match output to demand by following signals of supply and demand, or a belief in the system's inability to do so, constitutes a continuing issue that divides economic optimists from pessimists.

In addition, a Marxist would stress that the concept of anarchy applies to the larger irrationality of a system that may equilibrate supply and demand, but that pays no heed to the usefulness of the goods that supply and demand bring forth. The anarchy of capitalism is thus its carelessness, its crazy indifference to poverty along-

95

side riches, its absence of any sense of applied human reason. By way of answer there is the ironic fact that anarchy in both senses of the word—mismatches of supply and demand, and an absence of a "rational" or humane plan of production—has for years been the central problem of planned economies, above all that of the Soviet Union.

V

There are many subsidiary explanations of inflation that I have passed over in this effort to present a wide-angle view of the problem. For example, some part of inflation can be traced to the steady movement within all capitalist economies toward the production of services rather than goods—a movement that also places more and more GNP in low productivity, rather than high productivity, industries. There is also ample evidence that the pricing structure of the economic system is powerfully influenced by the oligopolistic sector of big business, with its rachet price movement (only up, never down), quite aside from the union-corporation joining of forces. Most important of all, I have not given central place to the monetary explanations of Milton Friedman. This is not because I have any doubt as to the importance of an increasing money supply in the inflationary process, but because I interpret this increase in money supply as an accommodation to other "real" developments that cause business and government to spend more. In addition, despite the significance now widely accorded to money, there is still no clear-cut temporal association between an increase in money supply and an increase in prices.

I want to add a word about runaway inflations, always a lurking fear. All the runaway inflations of which we have any record are the consequence of political collapse, as in the Confederacy after the Civil War, Weimar Germany, post–World War II Hungary, etc. Nations can experience extremely high rates of inflation—over 100 percent a year in some Latin American countries—without the population losing faith in the currency and resorting to desperate expedients, such as barter, or refusing to sell agricultural products for anything but gold or other real goods.

I do not think, therefore, that a runaway inflation is a matter to be taken seriously. That does not mean that the "idea" of such an inflation may not continue to hover as a great hobgoblin over the stock market. In all probability, the future course of inflation will be a wobbling upward course, with the inflation rate slowing down when the government takes heavy-handed measures, and accelerating when these measures (which may induce recession) become too onerous. Judging from the experience of the last ten years, it should be possible to learn to live with these inflationary rates, indexing most people's incomes so that there is very little redistributive effect.

Notes and Comments

VI

One reads speculations that the international economic
crisis will usher in a new hegemonic age—that of the
multinational corporation. I doubt it. A great deal of
the much discussed multinationalization of the 1960s
was caused by a highly visible surge of American cor-
porate investment abroad, aided by the open-ended
IOU system of the American imperium. With today's
depressed dollar this is being matched by a corre-
sponding rush of foreign investment capital to buy
"cheap" American industrial assets.

There is no question that we are entering an era in
which the horizon of large corporations will be increasingly global, thanks in large measure to the rapid-
ity of travel and the technology of information han-
dling. But there is also a growth in the power of
nation-states "against" the multinational, especially in
the underdeveloped world. The poorer countries need
the multinationals because these great companies serve
as conduits to introduce new technologies and to orga-
nize large-scale economic undertakings. But the companies can no longer assert their economic power with
the near-complete disregard of local interests that was
characteristic of the activities of the older multinationals who introduced plantations or built railways or
opened the first mines. Quasi-military, quasi-socialist
governments constitute more and more of the regimes
of the underdeveloped world. Where capitalism is the

98

official reigning ideology, it is authoritarian capitalism closely (and uneasily) allied with its own military. The multinationals are still very powerful, but increasingly they live on sufferance. The idea of multinationals organizing world production in a planetary system of "rational" design is a fantasy that overlooks the fact that men and women will lay down their lives to protect the independence of their countries, but not of their companies.

VII

The Rockefeller quotation is from E. C. Kirkland, *Dream and Thought in the Business Community, 1860–1900* (Ithaca: Cornell University Press, 1956), p. 9. The Samuelson reference is to his *Economics* (6th ed.; New York: McGraw-Hill, 1964), p. 113.

The more or less deliberate misrepresentation of the nature of capitalism is a much more serious issue in our times than it may appear. The class struggle that in Marx's day was conducted with direct onslaughts against workers has long since vanished, except in such barbaric nations as the Union of South Africa. The class struggle today is being fought on the television screen and in the schoolroom. Whether it is being won by the forces of business is hard to say. Expensive and clever talents are employed to make capitalism plausible, "friendly," and unthreatening. Awkward facts, such as the distribution figure quoted by Samuelson, are studiously ignored. On the other hand, there is the patently self-serving character of much of the advertising effort, the contrast between image and reality that is difficult to explain away, and the increasing cynicism of prevailing beliefs. This latter is unwittingly promoted, I suspect, by the absurd and smarmy pronouncements of corporations on their own behalf. The "contradiction" of advertising is that its incessant, contrived efforts to conjure up belief ultimately give rise to skepticism.

VIII

The quotation from Marx is from *Capital,* Vol. 1, Chapter 25 (New York: Vintage Books, 1977), p. 777.

Professor Gordon's hypothesis is set out in his chapter in *U.S. Capitalism in Crisis* (URPE [Union of Radical Political Economists], New York, 1978).

The Kondratief cycle has a recurrent fascination for Marxian economists. Its most recent exhumation (it has been buried many times) is in Ernest Mandel's *Late Capitalism* (Atlantic Highlands, N.J.: Humanities Press, 1975) The appeal of the hypothesis lies in the undoubted alternation of eras of buoyant capitalism with eras of relatively stagnant capitalism. The problem of periodization—why fifty years?—remains un-

100

solved. This is not, however, a fatal objection. No one has ever suggested a cogent reason for the periodicity of the standard business cycle.

IX

The arguments for the crossover points will be found in "World Oil Production" by Andrew Flower, *Scientific American,* March 1978. The Leontief input-output study is published by Oxford University Press as *The Future of the World Economy* (1977). For supporting data and arguments, see Lester R. Brown, *The Global Economic Prospect, Worldwatch Paper 20,* May 1978, Worldwatch Institute, Washington, D.C.

The advent of a tightening economic environment, with its accompaniment of stricter economic controls, raises the question of the political outlook. This is a matter about which I have written in *An Inquiry into the Human Prospect* (1975) and *Business Civilization in Decline* (1976), and I do not want to repeat myself endlessly. But a few words seem necessary.

For many people, the likelihood of a higher degree of government authority establishes *ipso facto* a threat of totalitarianism. This is not a fear to be cavalierly dismissed, for bureaucracies do expand and may eat away at democratic liberties. To my mind, however, the threat to democracy does not lie so much in the

extension of government controls, irksome or bureau-
cratic though they may be. The danger resides, rather,
in the underlying difficulties that have caused these
controls to be erected in the first instance. For the
tightening environment must sooner or later exacer-
bate the tensions and frictions that growth has historically served to alleviate. The fight over the division of
output, both within and among nations, must intensify,
if the size of total output no longer grows as rapidly as
before.

Thus, in my view, a critical question affecting the
political outcome of planning will be the use to which
planning will be put in giving vent to the pressures for
redistribution that the next half century will bring.
Here, all history leads us to expect that the powers of
government will be used on behalf of the rich, protecting the share of the upper echelons of society—the
so-called "middle" class as well as the truly wealthy—
from wholesale invasion from below, and maintaining
the treasure of the industrial world against the demands of unindustrialized nations.

Such a defensive use of government power may well
encourage resort to authoritarian, if not totalitarian,
measures. Yet, even if the pressures for redistribution
are heeded, the tensions and dangers of the long-term
future seem likely to push all socieites in a statist direction. That seems to me the blunt truth of the matter,
which it would be deceitful to present in blander fashion. The challenge for those who oppose the pathol-

ogy of totalitarianism is therefore to distinguish the abuse of power, which must always be fought, with its use to ward off or contain inescapable perils. It is not planning, as such, that will be the Trojan horse of democracy, if democracy perishes. It will be severity of the seismic disturbances against which planning was meant to safeguard us, or the unwillingness or inability of a society to make bold alterations in its institutions, while these can still be carried out through appeals to reason and by democratic means.

X

The periodization was suggested by Horvat at a seminar at Columbia University during the winter of 1978.

A closely reasoned analysis of the crumbling of the traditional ethic on which the "market mechanism" depends for its operation is to be found in *The Social Limits to Growth,* by Fred Hirsch (Harvard University Press, 1976). Hirsch makes the point that the "bourgeois" legitimation, and indeed glorification, of acquisitiveness have traditionally been the prerogative of the business, but not the working, class. We have applauded money making, with few exceptions, when practiced by "successful" businessmen. We have deplored the same motive when exercised by teachers, policemen, or coal miners. But the acquisitive ethic has

103

percolated down through society as one of the unexpected consequences of the triumph of the capitalist system. To no small degree, the Hobbesian free-for-all that threatens the stability of the wage structure is the consequence of the erosion of an older "I know my place" attitude, and its replacement by an attitude of universal profit maximizing, previously the prerogative of the business community only.

In the development of such "antisocial" attitudes lies a challenge to the maintenance of the capitalist system that cannot be quantified, measured, or accurately predicted, but that may in the end play a decisive role in numbering its days.

Index

Index

booms *(continued)*
  of 1950s and 1960s, 12, 79
  recessions following, 51
  see also crises
bourgeois democracy, 65–66
"bourgeoisification" (Engels), 75
Brown, Lester, 101
bureaucracy, growth of, 88
business cycles, 41
  impact on society of, 72–76
  Kondratief theory of, 76
  stop-go, 51
business failures:
  as consequence of recessions, 29
  incompetence and, 28
buying power, government policies
  and, 26

Canada, 39
Capital (Marx), 73, 92, 100
capital flows, international, 54
capitalism:
  crises and, *see* crises
  environmental issues and, 81, 83,
    84, 88
  institutional changes in, 76–77,
    79, 83–86, 88
  loss of appeal of, 85
  misrepresentations of, 67–68, 75,
    99–100
  modern vs. prewar, 42, 73
  moral issues in, 65–69, 75–76, 85
  national planning and, 79, 83–86,
    88
  proletarianization of, 74–75
  public sector growth in, 77, 78
  regeneration process of, *see* capital-
    ist expansion
  structural problems in, *see* struc-
    tural problems

  types of, 73, 87–88, 99
capitalist expansion:
  American hegemony and, 52–62,
    77
  breakdowns in, 27–37
  crises and, *see* crises
  end of, 88
  government policies and, 28, 42–
    51, 83–86, 88
  halt in, after 1973, 13
  Keynes's theory on, 40–41
  necessary processes for, 23–26
  oil crises and, 16–17, 20, 29, 57,
    77
  protected by economic planning,
    79, 84
  stages of, 18–22, 23, 29, 31, 34,
    91–93
  upward trend in, after mid-70s,
    14–15
  see also capitalism; growth
class structure, changes in, 74–75
communist nations, disillusionment
  with, 85
competitive capitalism, 73, 87
conservatives, 70
contradictions, economic, 51, 74, 84
cost-price relations:
  in boom periods, 30–31
  inflation and, 44–45, 47–49
counterprocesses, booms and, 29–35
Crash of '79, The, (Erdman), 15, 62
credit:
  government policies and, 28, 30
  in inflationary periods, 49–50
  in recessions, 71
crises:
  causes of, 16–17, 19–22, 23, 27,
    29, 31, 36–37, 38, 52, 57,
    64–65, 77, 88–89

Index

108

Index